Castle Tzingal

Castle Tzingal

A Poem by

FRED CHAPPELL

Louisiana State University Press

Baton Rouge and London

1984

Designer: Albert Crochet
Typeface: Linotron Galliard
Typesetter: G&S Typesetters, Inc.
Printer and binder: Edwards Brothers, Inc.

Grateful acknowledgment is made to the following publications,
where some of these poems first appeared: *Black Willow*, the *Little
Balkans Review*, and *Southern Poetry Review*.

LIBRARY OF CONGRESS CATALOGING IN PUBLICATION DATA

Chappell, Fred, 1936–
    Castle Tzingal.

    I. Title.
PS3553.H298C3   1984   811'.54   84-9716
ISBN 0-8071-1190-2
ISBN 0-8071-1203-8 (pbk.)

In memory of Joe Nicholls

Contents

The Homunculus   1

The Queen   4

The Admiral   7

Page   9

Astrologer   11

Report of the Envoy to His King   13

Song for Disembodied Voice   15

Queen Frynna Waking   18

The Admiral Ponders His Sleep   20

Astrologer and Page   22

Second Report of Petrus to King Reynal   24

Tweak to Petrus   25

Astrologer: After the Dinner   27

The Admiral: After the Dinner   29

Second Song for Disembodied Voice   30

Queen Frynna Dreaming   32

The Mad King   34

Queen and Handmaid   36

Final Report of Petrus   38

Astrologer and Page   39

The Queen   42

Homunculus   44

Epilogue: Song for Disembodied Voice   46

Castle Tzingal

The things I dream of are forever
Beyond my reach, sunk deep in earth
Or at a human height. Unlike all others born,
I was conceived with purpose, drawn up to plan,
And have a surer measure than a man.
It's s rarefied temptation
Could smudge my honesty,
And as for what *you* offer . . .

                                    Well, we'll see.

The Queen

Sing to the mountain, my dear one,
*   Where do you wander?*
The skies muffle over with cloud
*   And the seas founder.*

No letter, Marco, has come as you promised.
The linnet has retreated as the zone of sun
Fell south, the corn is gathered all in,
And early snow embitters the mountainside.
Yet I receive no sign.

My fancy portrays you lying broken
By robbers or horrid beast, and all bloodstained
Your mangled harp. Still worse,
New love may possess your mind
And you forget me, plying verse
To music, tuning compliments
To bluer eyes and brighter hair.
How anxiously I pace the battlements
And pretend to keep my eyes on
The shriveled gardens below
While watching the horizon.
Perhaps tomorrow shall bring news of you,
I think, and lay me down to sleep.
But this tomorrow comes on as empty
As the sky is deep.

*   How careless the song you sang me*
When the meadows overflowed with white clover,
*   How winsome the vow you made*
To be my true and pliant-hearted lover.

In Castle Tzingal I sigh long sighs
And wish I were a silly child again,
Nestled beneath my father's stout roof

And never stolen away to be the wife
Of an iron and fruitless man.
All I'd unremembered I remembered when
You struck the harp and sang the old old ballad.
Unbearable sweetness overcame my head
And heart. I gnawed my inner lip,
Recalling the voice of my gentle mother
When your voice lifted up.
I am not suited for the intricate gloom
And thorny intrigue of a blackguard time.
There is a child, a sunny child,
Who dances within my breast and combs
Her sunny hair and coddles a painted mammet.
In these bleak years I am defiled
By the drunken ambitions, the nightmare designs
Of a petty Mahomet.
I shall not bide here ever.
The poppy chalice shall ease my sorrow,
Or the river.

As the lone long wind unwinds
    Her bobbin of white thread
She sings a song rejoicing
    That she never wed.

I am a captive lullabye in a land
Of battlesong; no one here
Loves fair word or silken hand.
My mother had not fitted me to brave
The lurid terror of my dreams of knives
Or the labyrinthine whispers that assail,
Asterve my wits. Here no man walks;
But sneaks or stamps or stalks.
And no one tells a tale but the telltale.
And no one thrives here but the mad
Or guilty. I dare not confess
In chapel to receive assoilment;

The priest is but a spy.
All this world hates the good,
And I'm afraid that I
Will come to be of these and lose
My soul, dishonor my noble blood.

Sing sing the silver willow
That flourishes by the stream
Sing sing the pink mallow
Like a faint flame

The Admiral

Hear the soughing along the black wall
And turret of Castle Tzingal!
I foresee an icy winter this time out,
Deep snow and tempest and heavy seas.
God's mercy on all poor sailors who
Climb aloft in the bitter squall.
I remember how in the rigging we'd freeze
To stone amid the biting snow
Until the bosun warmed us with the cat.

None of that now for me.
All seasons now I lie in drydock
And count my medals and clean my braid,
Come down to luncheon mark
At eight bells, set my boots out for the maid.
I pull my final duty: to bore
The queen and court and visiting ambassador
With tales of seafights long forgotten.
I distract at table while the King
Observes, and deliberates on war.
An old man whom the smell of sea
Nevermore reaches, for whom the sting
Of saltspray is a darkening memory.

Young sailors, take warning.
The certainty of your hand deserts,
Your fresh blue eye grows blear,
And the snows of heavy winter
Lie less lightly every year.

Sleepless midnight, and the knobble bones
Keep revel down with ray and shark.
This North-whelped wind is a chorus
Of far-drowned sailors, groans,
Tears, and prayers flying in the dark.

I cannot sleep for all the tears,
For all the cries, of my drowned men.
I picture the foamsprent wave, how it receives
The tumbling snow and drives,
Drives against a lonesome reef
Its full freight of grief.
And I cannot sleep.
And the wind cannot stop.

I pull the foamy counterpane
Tight beneath my chin
And stare at the coffered ceiling
Until the dawn leaks in.

I would now put to sea once more,
Up anchor and away to the world's swift edge;
And over, sailing to the farthest star
That shines on the western verge.

But cannot.
Cannot even sleep, except to dream
Or half-dream the whirling eye of maelstrom
That sucks the ship, even the stars,
Into its sudden gullet.
And down I go, pulled splay against
The force invisible and unvanquished
That wrinkles the fabric of the world
And takes me steady as a bullet.

Heave, heave away, my lads.
We tack and turn into the wind,
And we sail blind
Without commission, chart, or polestar,
Into the world we leave behind.

Page

An't please you, sir, to step this way,
Maestro Astrologer will presently join you here.
Regrets, I am to tell you, his unlooked-for delay;
But my master is kept busy-busy in his tower.
So many calculations, so many requests
By such distinguished noble company,
That I'm hard put to find how he performs
All, and yet retains sweet equanimity.
But still it's certain he'll give ear
Considerate to your need most near.

May I bring wine? Or else to your comfort?
No? Then I'll withdraw within a moment's
Space, but first I ask you, sir—
If you will pardon my minion impertinence—
How like you this green doublet that I wear?
Because you travel broad, sir, and see the fashion
Of the greater towns and have most knowledge,
While I, indentured page, must keep here
In Castle Tzingal five years longer before
I gain my freedom, and have no way
To know how the fine world dresses out
Or how they do.

Why, thankee, master. Your kind words I'll remember
And treasure up for the dull days that lie
Before us here in this sour winter.
I do admit to being somewhat vain
Of this rich cloth, which Maestro Astrologer gave to me
For special service extraordinary.

I fancy, do you see, I've made myself
More valuable than the general class
Of manservant. I have intelligence
And am willing, sir; can keep my silence

And hold a triple-brass allegiance
To my betters. Not everywhere these days
Are found such steady qualities.
Perhaps you'll fasten in your mind my name,
Which, sir, is Pollio, and if it came that ever
You needed someone of my cut,
Then you might purchase my debenture.

—Oh no, sir, I'm not unhappy here,
But adventurous to roam the wider world;
It's the youth-blood in me, and curiosity.
But I'm no featherwit, as soon you'd see,
Were you my master. For I have a clever
Way with secrets, how to weasel them out
And noise them all abroad,
Or how to keep them quiet as a shroud.
In taking up my contract, you'd also take,
As 'twere, a nether history
Of Castle Tzingal, because my loyalty
Cements fast to my new employer,
And I do all and always for his sake.
You'd find me, Master Envoy, quicksilver-deft
At any use or task, in bedchamber or in foyer.

For there are matters, both of word and deed,
That here have taken shape and would have value,
If ever they be known outside these walls,
To rival principates; and all you
Ever could desire to know is in my head.
Please don't mistake me, I am not offering
To tell for silver the slightest shred
Of information. Pollio's no traitor.
But if it happen by chance or fate or
Long design that I become your man,
Why, then . . .
But now I'm silent as an ear
Because I hear without the door
The dusty footstep of Maestro Astrologer.

Astrologer

Immortal and unpierceable ignorance
Cloaks the movements of the skies.
Always more is surmised than known.
We have the bit of knowledge that makes us men
But does not make us more than men.
I tell you this before to ward off
Too-ready confidence. My science is not exact,
You cannot learn from me all you expect.

Now then, shall I cast your stars
And tell you somewhat of fortune to come?
You seem a solid man whom the fires
Of circumstance have tried; you have strong hands
And open features. Have you a dream
You'd want interpreted?
I pride myself the speech
Of dreams is almost never beyond my reach.
Or I can analyze the humors of your blood;
One drop will tell us
What simples will be best for you
At any hour, what medicines. We never know
What unguessed accident may befall us.

Or I can give advice, reading your physiognomy,
On how to conduct your affairs, amatory
And otherwise. But now I look
More closely, I think you need not much
Of that. Your strong demeanor commands respect;
You are a man marked by authority.

—So then, you approach me not for aid
But information of the harpist-poet Marco
Who stopped at Castle Tzingal a year ago.
There's little for me to say.
I'm slenderly inclined to music or poetry;

Sterner details must occupy
My days and nights. A courtier or a waiting-maid
Can tell you better what you need to know.
I deal in harsher counsel, military
And political, and have no hour left free
For lute or dance or ode.

I do remember the man, indeed I do.
Queen Frynna was much taken with his art
And with his presence. He's just the sort,
You understand, to please the giggly women.
But all that twitter is outside my sphere.
I am condemned to ponder steady
The knotted problems of peace and war.

—You say you've heard of frequent commerce
Between us? True, I made a promise
Of potions which I never compounded;
I traffic not in powders to be given secretly.
Though he kept asking, I stayed him off
Until he understood that finally
I would not satisfy him thus . . .

                              Now, if
You will allow me, I must return to work,
I find myself so busy-busy-busy.

Report of the Envoy to His King

For the eyes of His Grace My Cousin King Reynal, Untarnished
Regent of the Kingdom of Reynal, Most Excellent &c., &c.

Your Highness:
This Castle Tzingal and its surly principate
Is not well, Cousin; I shall never come
To love of it. Some dark infection
Shadows all its goings, and a grim
Pustule of rank humor mottles its complexion;
It is a ground of nettle, nightshade, and toadwort.

I'm always looked on as a spy,
Which is but natural. Yet each man here
Is looked on as a spy, no matter what
His station, rank, or history,
No matter his connection with the Queen
And King; in fact, the closer the more near
To sliding danger, to the unseen
Midnight hand. This kingdom lives unclean.

Of your nephew Marco, whose silent disappearance
I've come here to trace,—not much.
I have unveiled some puzzling hints
And know that he stopped here indeed
Last year, received the gracious encouragements
Of Queen Frynna. Whether he went on ahead
To Woland is unknown. What he did
Is still, in fact, the object of my search.

I pray he tarried here not overlong.
An ugly murk of treachery
Envelopes all who dwell here or come by,
And so pervades the mind that one is changed,
Perhaps illuded, bent strong
Against his natural temperament.
A lad devoted to sport in open fields, to song

And skillful love-converse, as Marco was,
Would have but villeyn company in this place
And much dour argument.

I feel a heavy louring as I walk about.
The sidelong glance, the snickered whisper, averted face
And nervous hand, the louche grimace
And oblique sneer—these are the common coin
Of social amenity. The fate
That brought our Marco here was not a happy one.

What misery—can you well imagine?—
To have to live in such a state,
And such a state of mind! I see already
How it has marked the Queen.
Her disposition, sweet and lively
As it must have been, is fairly ruined;
She bears her breeding like an open wound.

A fortnight here I find myself
Gasping for air like a man in mortal combat.
I walk the ramparts to breathe the clearing sky,
And mornings I willfully sleep in late.
I have a megrim that will not go away,
I dread the coming down of night.

Much is amiss.
Whether any of it touches
The object of my search I cannot say.
Marco's affections would not be for this place
Or for these folk. And I do admit,
Neither is the liking of your close and faithful envoy.
—When I have solid news I shall communicate.

> *Your willing and obedient servant,*
>
> *Petrus*

Song for Disembodied Voice

There is a music sings without a voice.
There is a beauty has no body.
There is a light informs the sunlight.
There is a cold and secret place.

Not even the frore and darkened walls of Tzingal can keep in
Music that silvers the wind with shadow.
I am a hidden singer without a throat;
The songs I sing may cause the chambermaids to weep in
Their sleep in the restless fulgurant night.
I have a song that sings of death as a meadow
Of polished daisies; another song
Of a waterfall the tears of youthful lovers;
A song to be plucked on the spider's lambent string;
A song that says the destinies of rivers.
I have five songs of penitent devotion,
I have a song as salt and lacy as the ocean.

But I have no blood or flesh or bone;
Am become the purity
Of breezetressed longlined melody
As silken-whispery as a lady's veil
And as transparent to the sun and moon.

A melody as changing as cloud-seam.
A story as dark and tangled
As the shoal of stormcloud the north wind mangled.
A music that ends in leaping flame.

Who could have thought that it would end or begin
This way, the singer dissolved in song?
That a murdering hand could lengthen the line
Of the lay, a sorcery hand make strong
Even past my death
The story I am compelled

To tell, and must sing on till it is told
In one unstopping suprahuman breath?

If there's a mercy in either of our lives,
In the one we count or that arrives
When our accounted days shut down,
It is that memory
Can broider the ode and elegy
With freshest pictures of the dawn;
Or turning sidewise upon itself indite
A wistful intimation of approaching night.

I have a sorrow that no tear can cool.
I know a ghostly bird sings out of tune.
I find the parts that never make a whole,
The broken halves that never join as one.

I'd make my song like the wind-tossed willow tree,
Promiseful-green and all a-lilt,
Its lissome strands interweaving light
As when the silver withes entwine as if spilt
From the corona of a fountain bright
With sun-spangle from a pleachy sky.

I'd make a song of maidens bathing in a stream,
Their flanks and shoulders white
And gleaming as new-starched lace,
A song of a garland of children fat
And dimpled spiraling toward heaven's dome,
A song about a lovesick shepherdess,
If I were free to choose my theme.

But Arcady is fled and gone
Until I rend the guilty sleep
Of Castle Tzingal and, like the sun,
Wither this black scheming up.
I am no more alive,
And all my murderers thrive.

I have a truth to say, no tongue to tell.
I know a heartsick prison without a wall.
A star lies silent in a silent well.
Not feeling cold, I live in coldest hell.

Queen Frynna Waking

What ribbed dark wings are over me?
What demon poised to swoop and snatch me up
Like carrion?—Ah no, now I see
It is the murky folds of canopy
Above my bed that greet me when I wake from sleep.

Yet that's a portent also.
My nights are full of portents; last night
Overfull. Bad dreams, of course,
That do not vanish with the light
I have become accustomed to.
But here was something else. . . A song
In a voice so dear
And yet so unfamiliar
It nearly broke my heart. It hung
So palpable in air
I dreamed I could as well see it as hear.

Or did I dream at all?
I am confused, as though veil on veil
Of cobweb were falling like snow to cover
My body and mind
In a shroud of tenderly restraining silver
That is the night I cannot leave behind.

What were those words?
"There is a beauty has no body . . .
There is a cold and secret place."
They bring no message I can piece to sense.
The message I derive is just that voice
That somewhere I have heard before, melodious,
And gentle when speaking to a lady.
It must be Marco's voice, brought hither on the winds.

Where is he then? In what drear habitat
Lies he enchained, enchanted?
The witches of Karok may hold him thrall,
Deluded by phantoms of gorgeous hot
Desire; or the sorcerer tribe of Moma in their haunted
Woodlands bind him in unbreakable spell.
Or he is prisoner
Of the giant Ghuras and his companion bear.

Still he is living, if this dream be true.
Shall we trust our dreams, then, for intelligence?
My mother dreamed that I should live a happy life,
But see. I'm glad she cannot see.
How may we trust a thought that comes we know not
    whence?
I am King Tzingal's half-mad wife.

"I know a sorrow that no tear can cool . . .
A music that ends in leaping flame."
The more I puzzle them together, the more
They fly apart, these words.
They settle and resettle like a flock of birds
Foraging the wheat; they tease
My consuming ardor
To know of Marco how and where he is.

Perhaps he'll come to me
When winter has passed over,
My pliant-hearted lover
Returning glad and free.

"There is a light informs the sunlight . . .
A melody as changing as cloud-seam . . ."
I do not trust myself.
I cannot trust my dream.

The Admiral Ponders His Sleep

Last night the worst.
Never more chilling, never more clear
Have the voices of my foundered sailors
Sounded in my dreaming ear.
Am I cursed
Forever to hear them dying in my sleep?
Am I condemned to watch their falling falling
Down through the gray deep?

Old age is upon me, and without its honor.
How shall I bear
Each night the ripping shrouds, the blood,
The youthful shrieks and cannon-sundered air
Without stark fear?

It seems their voices grow more wistful-tender
As my years advance.
Last night more plaintive still. No chance
They ever shall keep quiet, but grow and grow
Into unending thunder.
I must somehow make my own silence.

What was it that they sang?
"I have a sorrow that no tear can cool . . .
I find the parts that never make a whole."
Strange song for brave tars to lift
After death has enlisted them all.
Where are the lusty chanteys that used to drift
Among the gulls, where is the thumping call
To quarters? Their deaths have made them children,
They have forgotten they were men.

I am forgetting how to be a man
As the dream-torn nights undo me.
Shall I receive no grace then,

No forgiveness that may come to me?
Everything I did was in the line of duty.

I followed orders.
Engagements must be won
When that is possible, whatever the cost.
I caused no murders,
Committed no crimes. To the very last
I carried out my battle plan.
All commanding officers must do the same.
But what do the other commanders dream?

"A story as dark and tangled
As the shoal of stormcloud the north wind mangled."
I know that weather-sign.
It bodes high seas
And sudden storm.
Some shambling destiny has black design
Upon my latter years. My days and nights deform
Into slow disease.

Well, well . . .That too I can amend,
If the nights bring no release,
With my own hand.

Astrologer and Page

Pollio

Did you, Master, sleep well last night?
That I did not, I must confess.
Some troublous dream I can't remember held me tight
And shook my sleeping as a terrier shakes a rat.
It seemed all night I heard a voice.

Astrologer

Some love-phantasm, I have no doubt,
Keeps your weasel mind alert.
King Reynal's envoy visits here to spy,
And you become his catamite
If once I close my eye.
My Pollio's a savage little flirt.

Pollio

He has, I think, no taste for what we do.
He is but a stolid little man
And lacks imagination. Not the sort
That I'd send out as spy.
He hardly finds his way about the court.

Astrologer

Half-clever is what you are.
This Petrus hides his every thought
And impulse behind a sleepy diffidence.
You see the man as the man's
Strategy designs: a dullard blot
Of inconsequence.

Pollio

Then you've discovered his purpose here?

Astrologer

He seeks Marco, Reynal's nephew, and makes
No secret of it. That much is open to the world.

What else does he purpose? Does he think of war,
Of treaty, or of subverting plans? Tweak's
Our instrument to find him out impure.

Pollio
As always . . . I say I slept not well.
Heard you no singing in the night,
No shivery voice thin-edged with bony moonlight?

Astrologer
I heard the wind make music over crenellated stone;
Bad dreams wrought cries from the Admiral and
    Queen.

Pollio
And nothing else?

Astrologer
                    I heard a star unseen
Weep as it fell from its accustomed sphere,
I heard the bat and owlet squeak and whoop,
I heard the dark midnight rise up.

Pollio
You heard no singing, no melancholy plaint
That quickened blood and made all sense grow faint?

Astrologer
None of that. Which must be the call
Of the bad conscience you have and I have not.

Pollio
Because, Astrologer, you have no conscience at all.

Second Report of Petrus to King Reynal

Your Highness:
I have yet no solid information.
But something is afoot,
If I may trust the intimation
Of whispers and vexed gesture. Last night
There was a song that troubled the castle's sleep,
A song whose singer was unknown,
And made Queen Frynna weep.

It came from nowhere-everywhere
And sounded clear, though small,
In chamber, nook, and corridor.
It was as present with us as our own souls are,
Impalpable as moonlight on a wall.

It was such a ballad as I've heard Marco make
When dispirited, cast down
By misfortune in love, or when
A dear comrade fell in battle.
It was Marco's song.
Who knows the stamp of it will
Never be mistaken about its maker.
But was it Marco singing? That's unknown.
His voice is something like and something not.

Whatever the facts, that song has cast this court
Into deeper confusion yet.
Events begin now to precipitate
Their ends. And I shall give report.

Ever Your Majesty's ob'dt s'v't,
Petrus

Tweak to Petrus

So. You're back again.
Do you bear a more imaginative bribe
Than that you offered when
You first approached me? I hope
You've racked your brain for— . . .

                        You say
That under King Reynal I'd have a duchy?
There's a thought might cause my fealty to slip.

Astrologer laid perhaps too much quicksilver
In my genesis.
I'm *mercurial*, a rider of swift whimsies,
Changeable as cloud, but always,
Of course, a constant Tweak-lover.
So.
I'll tell you how it is.

Marco is dead. That is, he's mostly dead.
But a part of him still lives in pain and horror.
King Tzingal conceived a jealousy of the poet;
Gave orders for his murder.
And then with his own hand chopped off his head.
He ordered my father Astrologer to do it
With a burning poison, but reserved the harder
Pleasure for his own royal sword.

He fancied, you see, that Marco and the Queen . . .
Well, you need no pictures drawn.
And there was no truth in it, not the least,
But King Tzingal never inquires for proof. He's mad,
You know. His body is a cage, his mind a beast
Harried by phantasms of guilt, presences
No one else could see or know; the dead
And living inhabit his head

Equally, make equal speech and equal silences.
I hear it all at midnight, grinning beneath his bed.

You needn't flinch so sorely. There's worse yet.
The severed head still lives. And sees. And hears.
And feels. And knows.
And may survive for years and years,
Could live through uncountable centuries
Sustained in agony by means of Astrologer's art.
I know but little the process of these things.
Yet I know the severed head *still sings*.

The ballad that so distressed all sleep the other night
Proceeded from a grotesque undercellar where,
Suspended in fluids beside a gurgling retort,
The harpist's comely head sang all the hour.

This was of course a song not counted on.
The King designed this latter existence as a torture,
A silent one. Each dawn
Was to bring more weary sorrow, more disgust
For that quasi-life, to Marco.
He planned to kill the poet but not the man.
And now it seems the poet may persist
Though all his sweet humanity is gone.

So.
This then is what you wished to know.
—Nay, not what you wished to know,
But what you were commissioned to find out.
It's Tweak who told you, you won't forget.
Do you think your sovereign might find in me
Intelligent steward for—let's say—a modest duchy?
I never would contest for a more ambitious prize.
A modest *little* duchy. To match my size.

Astrologer: After the Dinner

The King was in rare form tonight indeed.
No one escaped his sulphurous insult
And bitter sneer and sullen threat.
Queen Frynna endeavored thrice to plead
With him, but only turned that ugly heat
Upon herself, the bellows-aggravated flame that yet
Shall wither us all. The Admiral, the Queen,
Petrus the visiting ambassador, myself, and even Tweak:
Each served with such snarling remark
As might vinegar the wine.

"Tell us," he told the Admiral, "how you took
Zomara, and what you said when they struck
Their colors. What joy
That victory must have been! Or were you—
As I have heard—below, buggering the pretty cabin boy?"
The Admiral stared unseeing into his plate.
"I know," the King continued, "of field commissions in battle.
But to raise a lad from lackey to First Mate?
I fear you take no prize for being subtle."
The Admiral's face, and even his hands, went white.

And when Queen Frynna tried to intervene:
"Quiet you, slut.
I know, as everyone knows, of your dalliance
With the prinking mincing jingling poet
Who sojourned here this twelvemonth last.
O, that was a quaint idyllic scene.
You'll trifle away your virtue for a song and then presume
To instruct me concerning best
Comportment for the royal personage? That alliance,
And your scranny hypocrisy, have made compact your doom.
Which I intend as bloody past endurance."

Petrus, our late-arrived envoy, ventured then
A remark to deflect that brimstone
Cannonade, but received the fury in full bruit.
"So now the spy from King Reynal makes speech?
Go back to tell my cripple half-brother
The kingdom of Tzingal is now and always beyond
     his reach.
I view his thievish purposes from afar
In time; I know before he knows of his pursuit
Of my envied crown.
Tell him it pleases me to carry war
Upon himself until the snowy boulders moan."

"Not war, Your Highness, surely not war,"
I said, "The counsel of the stars does not favor—"
He silenced me with a savage gesture.
"For you, Astrologer,"
He said, "all energies of life have lost their savor.
You are sick and cowardly and have betrayed
Some best part of yourself. Do you recall
The earnest scholar once you were and have since unmade?"
In boiling shame I hung my head.

Tweak giggled, and the King glared
Toward his table-end. "Scorpion," he cried,
"Insect, animalcule. Toad! Do you not know that—"
Tweak made a grimace and disappeared . . .

So passed a passing cheerful evening in our court.
In kingly sport.

The Admiral: After the Dinner

What will become of her, the good queen who tried
To shield me from King Tzingal's disdain,
His cruel insult? I revere
And pity her whose destiny will be sad
And harsh, harsher even than my own.
Her attempt to shelter me will cost her dear.

My fate is known to me.
I take it all in hand this night.
The sailor, however long from sea,
Still keeps his skill to make a knot.

And this night's injury is the last.
The worst, the last.
I have prepared to journey where degrading insult
Cannot reach, where force of dour contumely
Is lost.

I go to the bottom of the world to join
My broken ships, my swift and jolly
Seamen who went down before
In the smoke and wrack of war.
Make ready, bosun, to pipe me aboard below.
I face the cold headwind on the bow
Of this tall chair. I straighten the hemp cravat.
I step, and swing out slow.

Second Song for Disembodied Voice

"The tapestry itself unweaves and weaves.
The swallows cross against the sun,
Light and wind take force as one,
The snow dances the spiraling-down of lives."

Without flesh or bone or sense or nerve,
I am the disturber of the guilty castle.
The melancholy notes I sing I know not how,
And yet the song goes out, a throstle
Song that quivers hidden fears
And makes the blood course cold and slow.

I am memory that, though silenced,
Will never cease.
No midnight ease
Will ever come to the sour conspirators. The wall rinsed
With moonlight, the unwavering Great Wain,
The creviced mouse-squeak and soulful night breeze:
All these withhold the ached-for sleep past dawn.

Marco's become a monster.
He has a human head, a body of black alchemy.
I am such a centaur
The ancient legends never dreamed nor ever could.
But am I still me?
This is the final torture,
To live and know
I am still Marco.

"The stars hang over this place of death
Like butterflies that burn and feebly wing
Toward some great sphere of darkness swirling
Slow and dreadful above a withered heath."

Why have they killed the poet but preserved
His unanswerable duty to sing?

Why have they sheared the soul from the man?
No crime against humanity or God has yet deserved
Such unimagined punishment, no black sin
Received such frozen penalty.

Until a mad king dabbled in chemistry.

"The starry frost returns, the helpless flowers
Withdraw like frightened petitioners
Before an angry monarch.
The happy season of the world has left no mark."

So I live on, if live I do,
To wrinkle and pull tense the minds of those
Who have created me what I am now
Until a thorough justice arise.

"There is a music sings without a voice.
There is a beauty has no body.
There is a light informs the sunlight.
There is a cold and secret place.

"The tapestry itself unweaves and weaves.
The swallows cross against the sun,
Light and wind take force as one,
The snow dances the spiraling-down of lives.

"A melody as changing as cloud-seam.
A story as dark and tangled
As the shoal of stormcloud the north wind mangled.
A music that ends in leaping flame."

Queen Frynna Dreaming

My *"doom bloody past endurance . . ." "The happy season*
Has left no mark . . ."
Mother, mother, come comb my hair and twine
It into the long and sunny braid
And take me in your arms out of the dark
And give me the mammet that is mine
With its bright hair and funny head
And hold me in your arms warm as sunshine.
And make that singing leave alone our dream
And go away. . . Or is it Marco singing? O,
Is it Marco?

I have dreamed him in another dream
As lying bloody broken in a strange forest,
But now I hear his song no rest
Is in my sleep but only jagged dust and ragged flame.
And you, dear mother, waver and turn ghostly
As I reach out in dream and cannot touch
Your form and mumble hoarsely
After you who comforted these bad days so much.
If from my dreams you go away
Forever, why should I not die?

"O, that was a quaint idyllic scene . . ."

"The swallows cross against the sun,
Light and wind take force as one . . ."
My happy childhood is a little gray mouse
That hides away beneath the eaves
Where all these terrors hungry and mean
Cannot climb to harm his cunning little house.

"There is a music sings without a voice—"
O, is it Marco singing?
"There is a cold and secret place."

It must be Marco. And he sings
Despite his murderers, despite his grave.
But how does he give voice? What things
Can he know to sing about? That he is brave
Beyond his death I must not disbelieve.
But what can I believe, what may I do
To allay his spirit's sufferings
In that half-world that holds him slave?

It was King Tzingal's doing. He gave order,
Or his own hand performed the murder.

I do not want this knowledge that comes to me
In song-torn sleep, in weeping dream.
"A melody as changing as cloud-seam . . .
A music that ends in leaping flame . . ."
And so it must be true.
I know the song is true.

And so.

I will not stay
A thrall to Castle Tzingal. I will go away
Where Marco is and be with him
In my forever dream.

"The tapestry itself unweaves and weaves.
The swallows cross against the sun,
Light and wind take force as one . . ."
Sing, Marco, sing again.

The Mad King

I am the toads' great lord, hating the toads.
Under the snow are many eyes.
A legion of foot-slither must me surround.
The burning salamander attacks the raven-holt.
Every heart unsheathes its dagger now.
Fire.

Fear.
I am the great lord of toads, great load of turds.
I have framed myself more crafty now,
I am everywhere all eyes,
My mind and not the Queen's is halt
And spites these roar-red hours that me sore-rend.

I slurk and navigate the sour round
Of Castle Tzingal's treachery till the clock speaks four,
Command my minions, *Thou shalt not; and yet thou
    shalt.*
They grutch my word and start like toads,
Unknow my stratagem of flame and ice.
I am their monarch's monarch born anew

And never ever fearful to be said No;
That is the nayer's certain warrant to be ruined
To thumbscrew or the smashing of his eyes.
Thus shall I teach them fair
Obedience, these quashy toads,
Teach them *Eyes right* and *Double-march* and *Halt!*

Who was it slew the poet? *Halt!*
I say. *Arrest the man.* Is not a man, but king. Now
That's a different matter, if he be lord of the toads.
Unhand him then. I unclasp my wrist. All round
They stare amazed, they are furious with fear.
That hour will come when I shall gnaw your eyes.

Dare not glaur at me with malapert eyes.
I count the keys of donjon, keep, and hold
And will unlock the secret of the fire.
The stiletto moment is verge-nigh now
When I shall give the order to surround
Them, dash their brains and bones, these swollen toads.

Our future time is no holt of shadow now.
I draw my wise-eyes circle to surround.
And soon I'll sear with fire these lordly toads.

Queen and Handmaid

Melessa

I pray Your Highness slept this night sound.

Queen

Ill. I heard that song again, the sad
Ballad that rose into my dream
Like a strangely flowered vine, round
And round in my thought. Did you not hear? I seem
To hear it ringing still.

Melessa

There was a music I thought I heard,
I know not surely. There is much
To trouble us, milady. There is such
Catastrophe I know not how—

Queen

O, what?

Melessa

Our ancient friend the Admiral is dead.
By his own hand. No one can say why.
I saw, I saw—

Queen

O, Melessa. Dear
Sad Admiral! What shall we do? My
Dear, my dearest Melessa.

Melessa

I saw
Them lift him gently down from the cross-beam
And lay him on the tumbled counterpane,
On that whiteness, as if he were borne on foam
To some alien shore that I could not descry.
As if he were delivered to the sea.

But his face, his face, milady, marked such pain
And terror that I was much afraid
And hid my eyes and turned away my head.

Queen

Lay your head now on my shoulder.
And consider, Melessa, that our Admiral
Has bravely escaped the bloodsick insult and blade-edge
    rancor
Of this sullen Castle Tzingal.
He may be most fortunate of us all.

Melessa

I cannot think so.
I looked upon his face and know
Somewhat of the anguish that devoured his soul.
And now, milady, his immortal soul—

Queen

May be suspended in eternal peace.
We know little of the heavens' decrees
Except their mercy. Our certainties
Must end there, lest we presume
To make our mortal fear that God who makes our doom.

Melessa

Yes, milady.

Queen
                  But do not dry your tears
Nor cease your weeping.
We may admire him who reached his hand
To grasp eternity, but we cannot commend.
Most surely there are others who shall end
Their iron and broken heartsick hours
In like manner. This death the others
Teaches us to understand.
I think I understand,
And have a thing, a little thing, in mind.

Final Report of Petrus

Your Highness,
It is a present death to me
To report that our brave Marco is dead,
That paragon of youthful grace. My sympathy
For your hard sorrow you are assured of;
You know my nearly equal love
And know I bear a heart borhe down sorely.

Each dread circumstance I will report
When I return.
Enough to say that he was murdered,
And King Tzingal at fault.
Justice is uppermost in my mind. I shall suborn
His minion homunculus Tweak, that silver-salt
Subtraction of a man,
And he shall work our justice out.

I purpose the killing of King Tzingal,
Your bastard half-brother, as well
For the safety of our state
As for proper revenge. He has made it clear
That he intends quick war
Upon our lands and would take us in thrall.
Our olden tolerance of this king must now turn hate.

It will be done, and with what speed
Gold and guile may muster to the deed.
His dying must be hard and dread.

I close in sorrowful haste and with all feeling,

Your Petrus

Astrologer and Page

Pollio
I come, Maestro, to bid farewell.

Astrologer
You desert me, then, to go away
With Petrus—as I have said you would—
And pledge yourself in service to King Reynal?
I surmised that we would come to see this day.

Pollio
You have the advantage of the stars
To find the future, and of your wiser years.
But I am young and, as it may be, silly,
And a fop, as you have named me before . . .
Yet I must travel where my liking tells.

Astrologer
Then you travel wayward, willy-nilly
To a kingdom you know nothing of. To war,
Perhaps, or to dark prison walls.
You have no guarantee
Of Reynal's favor, no surety
In Petrus' love. Yours is but a dim futurity.

Pollio
Yours the same. For Petrus knows
And has reported Marco's fate and your hand
In it. Before the winter-end snows
King Reynal's revenge shall hasten on this land
And no conspirator evade
The sentence he himself has made.

Astrologer
If Petrus has received this sharp intelligence
I think I know the spring of it.

Our Pollio's a greedy little sneak,
Are you not?
And hide your serpent's belligerence
Behind your perfumed show of being maiden-weak.
—But for this cause they have no evidence.

Pollio
No evidence? Marco's severed head shall testify.

Astrologer
And so it might if it did still exist.
The angry acids have eaten it away
To imprecipitate essence, an invisible mist
My retort reduces to a drop of dew.
The poet now is one with nature's elements,
His song is sundered air and scattered in the winds.

Pollio
You think that later ugly horrors shall erase
The former? I believe
King Reynal shall not stay his justice
On advocate particulars, but swoop into Tzingal
With fire and sword, and nothing here survive.

Astrologer
Then would he be unwise. The stars give strong advice
Against such action, and ensure his full defeat.

Pollio
How often have the stars said right
As you interpret them?
I have no fear to grapple whatever fate
You foretell mine. I go to seek a saner home,
Petrus my mentor and I no catamite.
I hear no stars speak politics at night.

Astrologer
I taught you, gave you, everything. And now—

Pollio

And now I go.
Anywhere, everywhere. Why should I stay with you
And end up, like the poet, at your whim
A drop of alchemic dew?

The Queen

The poppy's silver dust spills in the claret
Like snow in a moonlight sea;
This is the dust of endless bitter hours,
This the draught of a prayerful timely
Death mossy silence underscores.
Voile cloud dims the opium moon. Near it,
A lonely star
Glows cool and fitfully
Declines, seeming to rise then droop again,
Toward the unabidable dawn.

Hereafter's unyielding doors fly open with this cup.
If I but take a sip
I shall have taken a queenly step
Within the burning threshold. There I halt and wait
Until my eyes accustom the huge light.

. . . It's none so bitter as I imagined.
A dainty taste of it suffuses my blood
Momently and makes my mind a drowsy flower.
If now my courage thinned
And I could bring myself to drink no more,
Might I not live wise, age-lined,
And content? . . . No.
I should become stark mad.

Better to drink the sleep I have prepared
And lay my wasting body down,
My ravaged soul,
And close my eyes to see my gentle mother again
And faithfully become Eternity's ward.

Shall I find Marco? I desire
To hear a last sweet ballad.

Sing to the blue mountain, my dear one,
    Where do you wander?
The skies muffle over with cloud
    And the seas founder.

The lone long wind embroiders
    Her delicate empearlèd shroud,
The azure butterfly shall kiss my mouth
    Now I am dead.

Now I am dead
Shall I find Marco singing in the vast cool fire?

No drop remains within
The cup. I have taken
My death solitary and polite
A little at a time.
And I embrace the night
I have longed to become.
And I am not the same
Though still I clasp my dream.

> *Sing sing the flowing willow*
> *That shadows the flecked stream*
> *Sing sing the pink mallow*
> *Like a vanishing flame*

Homunculus

I dance;
I gavotte and cavort
Like the sparks that leap above the bonfire
In an autumn field; I foot
A gigue and hop a light bourrée.
My partner cannot keep the time, must sweat
And slowly turn and hold me in his stare,
His wild and dying eyes. Too late
King Tzingal understands his royalty
That slips from him. *Now say,*
Mad King, how feels the raveling fire
That licks your veins? Is not this poison sweet?
Tweak finds this poison sweet.

I stole it from my sire-Astrologer.
Well I know the deadly compounds he designs—
Born as I was from a boneyard elixir—
Know their effects and how they melt in wines,
And which are opiate and dull the sense
By little and little, and other acids which can sear
The blood and breath with delirium pains
Until the life flees gratefully hence.

What's that you whisper? "I am lord
Of the toads," you say? Why then,
Your Highness, so you are if you desire.
Is this your final word,
Proclaiming an empty unarguable reign
Over harmless creatures? Am I your toad?
See how I leap and hurtle to a strain
Of music that sweeps my fevered head,
Music that sings like jubilant fire.

We take a bitter strange farewell,
Your Highness and I, going to new lives.
I cannot say my hate complete,
I have a fury I cannot tell
That with your agony springs up, thrives
Like a burly and unquenchable briar
That has put down monstrous root
And in due time shall pull down all.

I'm careful your last earthly sight is fire.
Do you hear what I say?
I take the flambeau here
And flame the curtain, and now the tapestry
That celebrates your coronation we see flare
Like the glory of holy martyrs. *Do you see?*
Or is your spirit gone to air
Already? *Do you hear me speak?*
I am speaking. I am Tweak.
It is Tweak who touched this final fire.

Epilogue: Song for Disembodied Voice

The starry frost returns, the hapless flower
Withdraws like a frightened deer
Into its woodland deep and dark.
The happy season of the world has left no mark.

The tapestry itself unweaves and weaves.
The swallows cross against the sun,
Light and wind take force as one.
The snow dances the spiraling-down of lives.

The stars hang over the plot of death
Like souls that burn and quaveringly wing
Toward a sphere of utter darkness swirling
Slow and silent above a withered heath.

A history as changing as cloud-seam,
A story as dark and tangled
As the shoal of stormcloud the north wind mangled.
A music that ends in leaping flame.